PACIFIC LIGHT

ALSO BY DAVID MASON

POETRY

The Sound: New and Selected Poems
Sea Salt: Poems of a Decade
Ludlow: A Verse Novel
Arrivals
The Country I Remember
The Buried Houses

FOR CHILDREN

Davey McGravy: Tales to Be Read Aloud to Children and Adult Children

ESSAYS

Incarnation and Metamorphosis: Can Literature Change Us?
Voices, Places
Two Minds of a Western Poet
The Poetry of Life and the Life of Poetry

MEMOIR

News from the Village

LIBRETTI

The Parting (Opera by Tom Cipullo)
After Life (Opera by Tom Cipullo)
The Scarlet Letter (Opera by Lori Laitman)
Vedem (Oratorio by Lori Laitman)

EDITED

Contemporary American Poems (in China)
Western Wind: An Introduction to Poetry (with John Frederick Nims)
Twentieth Century American Poetry (with Dana Gioia and Meg Schoerke)
Twentieth Century American Poetics (with Dana Gioia and Meg Schoerke)
Rebel Angels: 25 Poets of the New Formalism (with Mark Jarman)

PACIFIC LIGHT

poems

. . . .

David Mason

Red Hen Press | *Pasadena, CA*

Book design by Mark E. Cull

Library of Congress Cataloging-in-Publication Data

Names: Mason, David, 1954– author.
Title: Pacific light: poems / David Mason.
Description: First edition. | Pasadena, CA: Red Hen Press, [2022]
Identifiers: LCCN 2022026226 (print) | LCCN 2022026227 (ebook) | ISBN
  9781636280578 (trade paper) | ISBN 9781636280585 (ebook)
Subjects: LCGFT: Poetry.
Classification: LCC PS3563.A7879 P33 2022 (print) | LCC PS3563.A7879
  (ebook) | DDC 811/.54—dc23/eng/20220606
LC record available at https://lccn.loc.gov/2022026226
LC ebook record available at https://lccn.loc.gov/2022026227

The National Endowment for the Arts, the Los Angeles County Arts Commission, the Ahman-
son Foundation, the Dwight Stuart Youth Fund, the Max Factor Family Foundation, the Pasade-
na Tournament of Roses Foundation, the Pasadena Arts & Culture Commission and the City of
Pasadena Cultural Affairs Division, the City of Los Angeles Department of Cultural Affairs, the
Audrey & Sydney Irmas Charitable Foundation, the Kinder Morgan Foundation, the Meta &
George Rosenberg Foundation, the Albert and Elaine Borchard Foundation, the Adams Family
Foundation, the Riordan Foundation, Amazon Literary Partnership, the Sam Francis Founda-
tion, and the Mara W. Breech Foundation partially support Red Hen Press.

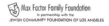

First Edition
Published by Red Hen Press
www.redhen.org

Acknowledgments

Grateful acknowledgment is made to the editors of the following periodicals and websites where these poems first appeared:

American Life in Poetry, Arena, The Australian, The Australian Book Review, Bristlecone, Canberra Times, Connotation, The Dark Horse, Forty South, Hamam, The Hopkins Review, The Hudson Review, Literary Matters, Quadrant, Rattle, Rosebud, Smartish Pace, The Times Literary Supplement.

For Chrissy

Contents

PACIFIC LIGHT

And meet it is, that over these sea-pastures, wide-rolling watery prairies and Potters' Fields of all four continents, the waves should rise and fall, and ebb and flow unceasingly; for here, millions of mixed shades and shadows, drowned dreams, somnambulisms, reveries; all that we call lives and souls, lie dreaming, dreaming, still; tossing like slumberers in their beds; the ever-rolling waves but made so by their restlessness.

—Herman Melville

On the Shelf

On the kitchen shelf a huntsman spider has left
its skin, which looks so much like itself
I thought twice before touching it. It was still.

The body left and left behind the soul,
feather-light and eight-legged, able to frighten
even when all it wanted was new life.

Perhaps you'll come upon my own shed skins
in houses where my name has been removed,
the habitations I once thought were home,

or find some words of mine in an old book.
I meant them. The words. Every one of them,
but left them on the shelf to go on living.

The Air in Tasmania

This green heart, afloat
in Earth's more-watery half,
bears like everywhere else
its lacerations, but the land
takes flying lessons from the air
and the air's great cleanser, the sea.

That cry in the near-dark
has yet to be identified.
Open the window and listen.
It comes to us
like the earliest memory
when we lay with no name
at creation. But the world is not
dew-wet and new. The continents
are islands too, dividing like cells
in a microscope.

Between here and Patagonia
titanic volumes of air,
the whorls and currents
cover the distances
known to the whales
and migrating birds.

We share it with bush,
the lizards, the fish, the green
rosellas coasting up to a limb—
from person to bird and back
to a person writing late at night
when the light of extinguished stars,
having crossed an even vaster sea,
can still be seen winking
in the same abundance
we are given to breathe.

The Lion on My Roof

Precarious days, vulnerable like me,
those months in a cabin in Colorado,
the thin walls, the windows leaking heat.

One night a lion leapt on the roof—I felt
the frail studs shudder at its weight.
Next morning half a dead deer lay in the yard.

A man's life is not a country's life
but I was broken open, losing weight,
and like America I was unsound.

Some days I was like that gutted deer,
a hungover face in the spotted bathroom mirror,
and when I hiked for relief in the dry hills

I was hardly surprised by the small arms fire
sputtering nearby. It was only practice,
but the sound of it, rapid and echoing, was all bile,

nightmare America shooting the light out,
so many weapons bent on killing time.
Give me the lion, I thought, hunting at night

from the height of a cabin roof, keeping herself
out of sight in the day, abiding the quiet.
Give me the wound I know I can endure.

•

I cannot remember boredom,
though must have felt it
on long summer days,
kicking the stones between
railroad ties, finding
the burnt lumps of coal.

Perhaps I was bored waiting
to be driven to movies
on huge outdoor screens,
movies too boring to watch
about men in cars or the lost
technicolor patrol—

one by one they were picked off
like minutes in a day
that went on and on
until the movie stopped it,
putting them all to sleep,
or I reached for the girl beside me,

strange creature, the fear
of going too far,
the fear too that she might be bored,
as the young are bored
on long days we never
wanted to end.

• •

Perhaps I was never bored,
but I knew betrayal,
my own and others',

and the absence of joy
that seemed of all things
most unnatural,

that I was becoming a block
worn down by the words of others,
the looks of others at work,
the judgment of others
known only too well
like the smell of exhaust

over the highway
exhausting the senses
days at a time.
I knew the dream-boss:
*Try to do better, try not to think
too much of yourself.*

• • •

The boy who cannot remember
ever being bored
is the man who endured
decades in the blink
of an eye, and is never,
not even by *nothing*, bored,

or by nights in which all creatures
are strange, and joyfully so.
I set out among them
with no need to know
the hour or any coordinates
on which our journey will end.

THE STORM COAST

In those years we lived so close to the sea
it never stopped its roaring in our ears.
The earth shuddered, its boundary overnight
scraped clean to lava bedrock or blanketed
with sand where shorebirds gathered in the dawn.

Our days were guided by those birds—the way
they understood the sun's astonishment,
the way the night rose up between the trees,
the way we came apart in sleep, the way
we stared at sea when the light came back, slowly.

We too were still and gladdened to be there,
cracked open by the elements like prayer.
We lived with no more shelter than a rhyme,
one measure of daylight tagging the next
till day was only the echo of the day

but with a difference felt along the skin.
The gimcrack houses and shops of America,
a thin and transitory way of saying home,
were pelted by the horizontal rain
the flow and tumult of the Ring of Fire.

I wonder if the sea will take that house
and fold and drown it like a paper hat.
What light it gave us, though. What years of peace
even when the storm blew clear inside us,
caught up in that coming in, that going out.

CROSSING THE LINE

She found the Earth online and showed it to me
glowing on a screen, and blue
the way I'd always thought I knew it:

crowded like so much thought with continents,
different-colored ink blots. Here are the steppes,
here the oil fields, the stains of poverty.

You see? You never actually knew the line
and never crossed it in your consciousness.
She turned the world and showed me the equator—

a line I'd never seen in my northern life.
Now look. The Earth is mostly water, like us.
An Andean narrowing to the Land of Fire

and then *Terra Australis*, the Southern Land
that Europeans took so long to find,
and next, across the Southern Ocean where

the albatrosses dream between the swells,
unwritten whiteness shrinking toward the pole.
She turned me upside down and brought me here

to walk upright under the Southern Cross.

THE VOICES

I came to a wood where dark trees were talking,
their voices sparking in the shadows, near
or distant, singly and in chorus, and I thought:

This is the way of trees, to wait until we least
expect it of them, then to speak from their depths,
the nerves strung out in lines with each new flash.

Black Mary died here, only twenty-one,
of fever.
    Wings. A rain-bright bird sank past.

This is the place of all things gathering, known

by no name.
    You too are known by no name.

Hear us talking. We are not unlike you.

There a boy died, native of Van Diemen's Land,

there a soldier, soused, holding a pig's head.

Women's voices, voices of men, the solitudes
of trees distinct and intertwined, and all

cast out in the darkness, with a full moon
blurred low on the cloud horizon:
      Who are you?

I have come too far to turn away from you.

Migrants, natives and indentured souls
alike were talking in the dark, each flame
an instant dying like a distant star.

And then I knew this forest was my home,
that I was welcome here among the lost.
This was the peace of all untethered lives,

even those who never found the words.

Dusk when the people in the trees
stand out against the dark—

it isn't dark, only a deep gradation
of the light—

the people in the trees,
crone-like olives,

have been gathering all day,
raveling and unravelling their hair,

their knotted fingers,
tableaux of maenads, harvesting.

Even on the other side,
the over-underside of the globe,

even here it is not dark but only
a deep gradation of the light.

The eucalypts are people,
dusky-skinned, composed—

they are not people, you know,
though we resemble them,

less stable in our steps,
less able to withstand the wind,

whatever wind we think it is
that tears us from each other.

Our hands are knotted too, our skin
spotted and scarred,

the birds in our brains can learn to sing
and spend their whole lives practicing

the change, the measure of light
and deeper light, the spill of stars,

planetary whispers—
what is it? I can barely hear—

A WORD

Some words can touch the things we want to say.
This morning, *dew*, or as the Greeks would have it,
drosiá, a cooling word, suitable for morning.

So take your coffee in the dewy shade,
receive the kiss of morning and return it.
Delay the job, the fretting over money.

Your mouth is open to the word, *drosiá*,
the skin of morning in the moistened air.

Drosiá, drosiá, like the beloved name,
the damp cool skin of morning and our love.

THE WORK

Time is the hillside falling away in grass and gum trees,
the current of water, the island behind the cloud,
and there is more of it and less of it than we know.

The striated bark of the peppermint gums, their smell
after rain, the early light just now touching the tips
of the grass like low-banked coals warming the world.

Once, work was the thing one rose to by the clock,
the place one drove to, the faces one met getting coffee.
Now there are stones to be moved, but will they be moved?

I have felt as others feel a quiet terror
yawning like a black hole between the trees
where matter falls in and never returns.

We are doing the work no other demands in the light
we are given, forgetting what day of the week it is,
the work all other work was a way of putting off.

LONG HAUL

In airports everywhere I see
people I think I know.
Someone I used to be married to,
someone who's dead now.

That one I wrote about,
and blush at what I said.
That one I met at a conference—
no, he too is dead.

I had a friend who looked like that
when we were twenty.
If I spoke to him I'm sure
he'd tell me plenty.

Another looks at me as if
I'm a familiar ghost
then turns away, discarding me
among the rest.

And when we fly, the earth below
and all identities
are cloud or glimpses of the sea
or blazing cities

in the dark, our wing a blinking eye
until the clock unwinds
the dream, until the dream unbinds
all that is passing by.

THE LOVER MAKING TEA

There is relief in darkness,
morning rain, the wattles
nodding their blooms outside.

Winter stirrings. Late July,
the sun rises in the north
and crosses low the southern sky.

This day the rain, the dull
glaring roofs of an island town
hunkered but at peace.

Rest now to the traveler.
Go in, go deeper in
where the soul resides.

The soul too is a cold dim light,
watered by the rain
and ready to unfold

the way a town at morning
barely breathes and stretches out
and makes small sounds of waking,

the way a lover makes the tea,
small stirrings, waiting
for the dark to steep.

LIVES OF AN IMMIGRANT

. . . is 't not all one to fly
Into another world, as 'tis to die?
—John Donne

A wren lifts off in one hemisphere and lands
in another where the pages of a notebook
fan and foreign trees are turning in the wind,

a strangeness one could wake to anywhere
with mountains that resemble mountains, sea
resembling sea, the waves like pages turning.

This is the way I cross to another life.
I thought it was a place, but it was time,
a depth of trees I look through to the past.

The notebook in the wind, its every page
a clutter of impressions, crossings out,
restartings, failures, blots and silliness,

is like the dull arthritis in my hands
a living twinge, and it will lose one day
all feeling, becoming what I can't describe.

We have to leave the world before we know it.
Losing a country or giving up on one,
is nothing but another form of death,

the dying we prepare for every day
but will accomplish wholly unprepared,
our notebooks blotted with incompetence,

our pages ruffled by the wind or turning
slowly into soil with other matter,
the lives and passports of an immigrant.

•

Why did you leave? Not at the point of a gun,
not as a refugee. To cultivate
a new relation to the world, and love,

the simplest of motives, so to leave
was not to lose more than I would lose
by staying still. To choose the given day.

To work beside my love. To watch the wren
feeding and playing as pages fan in the wind.
To see the Southern Cross, the Milky Way,

I've gone to school again. Learning to speak
without offending beauty, I have lost
the language I was born to as I must,

learned to be stirred by sagg and eucalypt.
My skin would feel the same in any country,
nothing here I'd not mourn anywhere

love anywhere with the same gratitude,
the same nostalgia for the present life,
the places we incessantly misplace,

the voice that sends us looking for a face
in waves and mountains and the bark of trees
the mind an ark we send out on the seas.

PACIFIC LIGHT

for Murray Ross

At the end of a winter day, the light
beyond the lighthouse point is turning fatal,
glittering far out, or closer in the manes
flung back from waves caught in the act of breaking.
It fills the room and thins to bleeding out
until the colors heighten. It streaks the salt
where windows frame a half-occluded view.

I remember now. The light in my mother's house
above a bay, a virile western sun
bleaching the spines of books, fading furniture
and making the candles we lit at dinnertime
doubly sad. I've watched for sixty years
the sun on western water, islands, clouds,
the mud flats, oyster beds and fishing masts—

the light I thought a poem should be infused with,
the light a man might die by in his bed,
the light remembered women leave behind
and children recollect like broken dolls,
the light destroyers cut with their gray prows
in my father's war, light the lava died in
with massive gouts of steam, and spouts of whales,

light in the cedars, redwoods, spruces, firs,
car windows flashing from the coastal roads,
light in a woman's hair, the campfire light
of surfers turning back to watch the waves,
the silhouettes of harbor seals, their eyes
haunted in dark sockets, lightless, watching,
light the dead will never see again,

and the living dead will never apprehend.
No pill or whisky and no burning weed
can touch the light, nor can the blue flame
of the struck match or lightning's jagged stroke
that sets the woods aflame. A passing light
that holds us watching motionless as seals
till night returns us to our element.

THE CONDITION OF MUSIC

Called to the door, we found a flatbed truck
loaded with opera singers, caroling.

This happened on the night my mother married
in Seattle. Many who had been friends were now,

by virtue of this winter celebration,
family, and in the city's Christmas lights,

the sheen of wet streets, in houses rising
above us, tier on tier into the night,

red silent stars of passing jets, our breaths
as we joined in singing, all of us floating

on champagne and love of the old words
that must in some dark world have been believed,

we wanted song, and were nearly fortified
for all the suffering that was yet to come.

Table Mountain

Stone and wood, a Forest Service cabin
smoked like a winter carol. We children leaned
from the sleeping loft to watch our parents glow

like demigods in whisky-colored firelight,
their snug laughter making a winter crèche.
In those days even nonsense words were meant,

the speech of love upheld the very night,
and we were pillowed by our frosty dreams
where animals tracked in starlight over snow.

I can hear the rock fall in that silent valley
crack like a rifle shot. The spell is broken.
Follow the small tracks melting under firs.

I never want to be a child again.

THE FIRST SEA WAS A SOUND

The first sea was a sound. Islands floated there.
Cook missed them altogether in the fog
veiling the strait, and sailed his *Resolution* on.
I recognized the wanting to remain unfound.

Once, I sank a line and reeled a furious
cod from a kelp bed. It shook free of my hook
and shot back to the watery underworld.
I felt its weight

and then I felt the freedom, weightlessness
and light where once had been a writhing fight.
A sound—and then a smell of gasoline
and brine and what the tide brought in,

translucent filament, long cuttings of mesh
and silver logs like bones of dinosaurs.
Intimate and other, called forth into
being and sent back . . .

The Written Snow

Muffled and dark, the blue hues
and tracklessness—how we went out
to watch the lightly falling snow.

Egalitarian and cold,
the taste of it, wet on the tongue,
compactness or looseness or kernelled.

How it stopped us, changed us, caught us up
without struggle in an apt surprise,
and then like everything grew old

and tediously gray and unwise,
shrinking into the shade, then gone
to bring about the revolution.

Once it was not to be endured
but loved bodily, the way we slogged
in it, the way our words were slurred

by laughter puffing out in fog.
Weather of pure being, gravity,
wet through but hot with play.

Night was a season of waiting, day
all melting angels, snow grenades
and gloriously cushioned tumult.

For some, of course, it was hard work,
the small fire snuffed out by snowfall,
the opened tin and the heating bill.

I mention snow for its own sake,
not having seen it for an age,
snow as memory, as blank page.

H. M. S. *Discovery*

Ghosts, glimmers, guesses—
the face in a yellow sou'wester
peering at the window
only long enough
for me to shout it out.
My brothers turned to look
but it was gone forever.

The water rat or otter,
some long agile thing
shooting under the dock
that autumn morning, chilled
between the rain and frost.
We looked and looked but never
saw the same shape again.

And those pale blue veins,
rivers of life that ran
beneath the near-white skin,
the nibbled aureoles
a destination of blood.
Hers the first I fondled,
greedy in my hunger,

the ship *Discovery*'s voyage
uncovering skin and steering
the hands, the tongue, the lips.
That friend's as gone as the face
in the yellow cap, otter
of mystery, surface light
hiding its long glide.

The End of Stories

I used to know his name, the fisherman
who chainsawed a skylight in my mother's roof.
Not your ideal tenant, she dryly said.

I knew he dealt to high school kids, and led
the life of someone people thought was cool,
a name at parties where I never went.

So that was who he was—a leaky roof,
one legendary season on a boat
and final buying trip to Mexico

where all the storytelling thinned to silence
or fell out, headless, on a desert road.
New stories rose, and someone else's weed

clouded our nights until the fire went out.
I couldn't stand the stuff and gave it up,
resealed the skylight in my mother's roof

and slept beneath it and the summer moon
and all the lunacy the country offered.
The end of stories comes for everyone

but not for stories. They go on living,
out somewhere, under a light of their own.

BARRA DE POTOSI

Well before the sunrise,
the fighting cocks start croaking
up and down the village of Potosi.

The tropical almond leaves are curious shadows,
outlined like elephant ears as light
fills in the world beyond the window,

then they are leaves with pithy fruit among them
as dogs join in the untuned chorus
with grackles and a starting truck,

a drumbeat from a radio, and I
step out, having heard the surf all night,
plosive and explosive, old earth-shaker.

Already on the lagoon men pole their boats
and cast their circles of net,
the pelicans make their spastic plunge for fish.

Sleek-winged kittiwakes and hunchbacked vultures
crowd the sandbars, taking professional interest
in everything that's in.

Women sweep the compact dirt of the street.
Their children play in the dust. Their livestock
wander like citizens with voting rights,

moving in time outsiders only dream of
as if to remember how we used to live,
how we might live again if the hours

were not wheels-up already and in flight.

New Geography

The land's prow aims for the Southern Ocean
beyond the port at Dover, beyond the tip
of Bruny Island where the lighthouse stands.

And then one thinks *beyond*. What heaves to mind
is league on league of rolling dreams until
the polar ice.

                An island's like a ship.

At night one fastens on the Pointer Stars
and finds True South, drinking the Milky Way.
Then gouts of rain, a sudden frenzy of air.

The morning is a windbrushed palette of bush
gripping the clay and rock from the last fire
to a dawn like the first dawn ever to be seen.

This little room looks out through gum and she-oak
to the sea. These brief inaugural jottings down
are cast out to the living powers here,

the things I've yet to learn of blood and fire
where the sea and river throw their lot together.
A life accumulates like water, dies

like air caught up in all the swirling currents.
Time to discover time as time once was,
seasoned and insatiable as always.

LETTER TO MY RIGHT FOOT

When I felt you buckle under me, heard the crack
of the ligament snapping and lay on the earth,
I hardly knew who to blame.

Just when I thought my body could do all it needed,
you said, *No, slow down, you're not*
who you think you are.

And now I must learn to do almost nothing.
From lying grounded I've moved inside
to the view at my bedroom window,

you propped up on pillows, my bed strewn
with laptop and books. I suppose
I should thank you for this.

Your hale twin must wonder what has gone wrong,
lies on the left beside you, eager to play
but obedient as a lap dog.

How brimful the world can be without my effort!
Rain has striped every peppermint gum
conducting the wind at my window,

the shades, gradations and tatters of green in the mist
deepen my seeing through to the far ridge,
and the blue of an island beyond it,

and the wise birds make their swift appearances.
How long till my body is thinned out in song?
Is this what it feels like, approaching

the last breath of a lifetime of breathing
and thinking and working
and filling one's days?

Dear foot, old friend, I've no one and nothing
to blame for the fall and the pain.
We're not parted yet.

You gave me the great honor of walking in the world,
and the trial of lying still in this raft of a bed,
this eyrie of being.

An Anniversary

The engines of the salmon farms are droning
faintly over sagg and gum trees, paddocks
and the silver-white of water brimming sky.
At its broad mouth, the river has lost all force
like an old god giving herself to the sea
as the sea wonders what will become of us.

We live at the nub of this history, told
and untold, known, unknown. Long before
there was a road this far, a ferry docked
at Pick-Up Point, churning north to Hobart.
At Oyster Cove Mathinna died, not last
but nearly last of an entire universe.

Or choose another anniversary:
surprise attack, and the American fleet
burning and sinking in the mid-Pacific,
my father's class rammed through Annapolis—
that mass of human effort, that steel fury
shrinking the globe and still unknowable.

The kookaburra's laughing. You don't know
and I don't know and all we can do is laugh
at history's hysteria. Pick up the tale
at any date and feel its animal writhing.
Dare to make a story from its cries
or lie down like a river meeting the sea.

PINE NEEDLES IN SNOW

As we have always known, the journey is all,
luck to the traveler, luck to those who stay,
for the road to the deep north is a narrow way,
and the name we give to autumn is the fall.

That a people of propped trees and waterfalls
could plunge their bayonets into the living
no history explains. Our thoughts are riven
even in a gentle painter's scrolls.

When the destroyer dodged a Japanese torpedo,
my father saw the passing pilot's face.
Then he came home. He found another place
of quiet rain, pine needles in the snow,

and built a garden with a bridge of wood
arched over water, and called his new life good.

Salvaged Lines

Having stowed our bags below decks, we stood
at the stern and watched Dutch Harbor recede,
Bunker Hill and Bally Hoo, the relics
of an old Aleutian war, the Russian church,
the village with its river—discontinuous
histories in some mad painting we had lived in.
There were masts of ships the Japanese had sunk,
and there the modern fishing fleet was humming,
the cannery barge was steaming, we were fleeing
like a band of non-compulsory refugees.

Then it was night on the open sea, the sea
no empire ever fully comprehended,
the sea that shuddered ashore with all the wreckage,
provinces of whales and seals, the many islands
too windswept for trees. Heather knolls, grass,
ptarmigan in camouflage—that was all behind
and we saw night and the first dawn without land,
and the storm ahead like some impassable wall.
Then we were in the wall and it was us.

A crew still has its tasks, like engine watch.
The below-deck porthole like a washer's eye
tumbling the sea outside, which left its salt
in wet drools on the glass. I'd check the gauges,
trying not to lose my lunch as the hull
churned like a carnival ride. Now I saw sky
bereft of gulls in the blast, now a trough
between dark swells scaled with smaller waves.
The air I breathed was oil. My brain was lead.
I marked time till I could climb to the bridge
and breathe the ice for a change, our white bow
rising and falling, a roof in a slow quake.

Where were we sailing? To another island.
What was our purpose? Nothing we could say.
How long would we stay there? Till it was done.

That was my time at sea. The names of shipmates
have blown out like old flags on the storm's wall,
the ice has melted from my beard, and I
have lost the notebook where I wrote it down.

If you are listening, no need to tell us
what you hear. We know the rifle shots,
the sputtering canisters of gas
and the other gas that makes a small girl
or boy dance giggling in the house.
We know the sound a cow makes
scratching her back on a low branch,
the scratch of a crow's call, the *woof*
of its wings in flight, the sea receiving
a pelican's hell-for-leather splash,
the daughter laughing in her mother's arms
just now, guitar and ukulele
finding each other's tunings.
We know the illusion of silence
that hangs between us in the night,
the bar fight staggering to a stop,
the stopping bus, its wheeze of brakes
and rattle of opening doors,
the thump of a wallaby's tail,
the nearly-dinosaur sound
of bison chomping grass,
the symphony, piano solo
from an open window, love
crying it's "I" out, sirens
ecstatic with emergency,
beggar's curse, rumble
of traffic. The awkward chord
kept hidden in a practice room,
the new attempt and the one
after that, and after that
the head bent still
over the patient instrument,
that breathing you can hardly hear
clouding the patient's mask,
the sound a tree makes

when the wind takes it,
the way the sea becomes a forest,
the forest a sea, and the same
for everything inside us
going further and further
from what we call the light.
We know the speed of fire and water,
and we know too
what it means to listen,
really to listen
when another speaks,
which may of all things come
closest to love.

THE SOLITUDE OF WORK

Unscrew the hatch and look down in the hold:
ten thousand purple crab in a living cast,
clicking the air with slow claws or clinging
to each other's horny shells. In boots and gloves
I'd stand on their backs, bend down and throw them
two at a time into the lowered mesh,
two hundred to a bag to be hoisted away
and kept alive in the sharp brine of the bay
till it was time to butcher them. That job
was harder, breaking a ten-pound crab apart
on a chest-high blade. They sensed death coming
and slowly fought the blade with claws like fists,
and when their shells were gutted empty things
thrown in a grinder, there was still a smell,
my own grim smell from a day of taking lives—
never a very happy enterprise.

So much happier was the hold cleared out
and hosed, where I sat in my own sweat and gear
feeling the sky rain softly through the hatch,
and work was done. My body reeked and ached.
The crew came down, bringing along their talk
and strutting lies. Somehow the solitude
of work stayed with me through the many years,
the many tasks left incomplete, the days
lightened in the forgetfulness of work.
The way I screwed the hatch back on the hold
and looked out from the deck on the dark bay.
One boat moved on, and another came to moor.

A Cabbie in America

He was from Rwanda, from Senegal—
there had been much motion in his life.
And did he miss his country? All
the time, and yet he lived here with his wife

and children, who were very good at school.
I said I'd always dreamed of Africa
and wondered if he thought me an old fool
for saying so. *No, no,* but it was far.

So many things were far, so many things
we wished for for our families
were far. And we were men, not kings.
He'd spoken French since he was three

and now the French was also far,
his tongue was struggling with American.
Once, he too wished to be a writer.
But couldn't he go to school again?

It's not too late, I told him as I paid
and finger-signed his little screen.
But how did I know whether it was late,
or half of what this gentle man had seen?

Rhapsody in Blue

To say it began at dawn is not quite true.
It began in the struggle of night escaping dreams
when the bounded world encountered infinite space.

Out of doors the shyest creatures moved
under the high holy vault and Milky Way,
bringing their young to the fresh grass, the spring.

The night was blue and the unblue moon rode high
in a calm sky and the gum trees hardly moved
and the dreamer tossed in his blue Doona, turned

in the lathe of his wishes and fears. And when he woke
his own branched hand bent toward him in the sun
streaming through the gums from over the hills.

Blue filled him then, from his eyes to his spine,
an inlet of sea he followed with waking eyes,
an island rising and falling, waking and sleeping

all the way out to the Tasman Sea. Next stop,
forever. Next stop, the albatrossing swell,
the seal rocks and dolphins weaving in the waves.

To rise in the blue world is to fear for its dying
and cling to the one day like a shipwrecked sailor,
remember the distant sneer of politics,

unending sneer and grimace, the demagogue
and the mob, and the *burn it all down* mentality,
a static in air, a crackle of codes blown clear

where the swallow leads the eye in an upward curve
and the cockatoo scratches the air and the air goes soft
and it scratches and softens above the fairy wrens

feeding in the grass, for there is work to be done,
there are stones to be moved and there is only a day
this day of the endlessness, day of the blue.

The Birthday Boy

The soft air, by this inverted calendar,
is still December, a day in early summer.
We're turning toward the longest day of the year.
Elsewhere the streets are narrowed by the snow
while here the sky is blue as a fairy wren.
I have no role in this, but I can thank
the fates for giving me this day, this life.

To have lived a while. To be looking out
from the green of our hill home to the sea
on this blue day. A book and a cup of tea
and no great hurry to get to any chore.
Even to say so calls up Atropos
cutting that thread of self—the birthday boy.
I'm held here by the stories I could tell

to nothing but the air, the trees and water.
Einai ola tyche, the Greeks would say,
and luck, all luck, is in the letting go.
I'm not the one who knows why I'm alive,
or why my body's not in pain just now,
or why the woman working at her desk
chooses each day to join her luck to mine.

We have come far. We're not alone in this.
There have been storms at sea. There have been tears
and there will be more tears. There have been days
I could have felt the dark flash in my brain
(and I will feel the dark flash in my brain).
There has been mercy and there has been rain.
I read a book that justifies its art

in every line and sip the tea and feel
the sunlight glowing in my bones, my skin.
I am the birthday boy, enlarged to nothing,
absorbed by everything the daylight offers.
This is the sort of thing that makes men kneel.
Consider me then, down on my old knees,
and this the benediction of an hour.

HIS PRISON

His was the best of prisons. He was free
to stay in place, in solitude
with one he loved nearby.

No one bothered with a lock and key.
No one told him he was bad or good
or whether he could or couldn't fly.

He couldn't, except that he could be
surprised by anything that flew outside his mood,
by anything that caught his eye.

The rain that fell from fern and tree
and turned the dirt road into mud
reflecting in its sheen the sky—

two vital spheres he lived between,
that were themselves a kind of bread
of solitude, taught him that he must die.

And death is every day's eternity,
the blessing of a friendly word,
the smallest gesture in reply.

The Widow at 102

She remembered cedar stumps that twenty men
could stand on, remembered how her hair stood up
when she sensed a cougar stalking right behind her,
but she could not quite recognize this girl
who sat beside her now without a story.

How many horses nibbled from her hand,
how many buckets of coal did the furnace burn,
and where was the lumberjack, where the saw,
the old trail in the woods like a dent in dough?
From one pale cheek a root-like tumor grew.

Thousands of mountain sheep were crossing the tracks
when the train steamed down the pass. The trees so tall
a storm was just a whisper in their topknots.
The rain fell like tea from the alder leaves.
The tumor, pale and waxen, rooted from her face

into the cool subsoil of the peopled air,
and everyone she knew was gathered there
the way a waterfall will find a pool.
Becoming root, a pale and searching thing,
her mind had found the water of the world.

THE SUICIDE'S HOUSE

Their faraway air—short stature, accents,
manners and reserve. People called it strange
that a Jew would marry a German, but wasn't he
a German too? The way they said *Welcome*.
The way they said *Volkswagen* or *schnapps*.
The way he read a newspaper, the way she
invited us children in for gingersnaps
and milk, her Grimms' Fairy Tale eyes smiling,
creased with sadness. The way he held himself
apart from people, and never fully joined
in the sort of talk the grown-ups said was small.

Their children were adopted. He sent money
to Israel, but would not talk of politics.
They lived in far northwest America
as if escaping history. One by one
they died, the father first, a suicide.
I saw him in his summer bathing trunks,
looking like Picasso, reading a paper,
his lawn chair in shade on the sunburnt grass,
then never again, and Lotte his wife
had even sadder eyes until she died
and the son died drunken in their Buick,
and the daughter moved away. She died too.

Now I'm an immigrant, I think of them
when I walk barefoot on dry summer grass
or come upon that painting by Cezanne,
the lane leading down to an empty house.
When you leave a place for good, sometimes you walk
in memory by homes you used to know,
as if rehearsing for the role of ghost,
severed from all ties to time and place,
the faint impressions people leave behind,
especially those of us who have no children.

I see their house hidden in Douglas firs
and walk past all the other houses there,

where strangers are unloading groceries
or putting screens in windows, or sitting out
on lawns and staring flatly at their phones.
There are so many lives we'll never know.
I'd tell them *That is the suicide's house,*
but whether it was money or the fate
of others in the camps I cannot say,
only that his wife was kind to children,
gave us cookies and never seemed to mind
the noise we made when playing out of doors.
I never heard them speak in anger, never
saw them weeping or lifting a fist in rage.
They came into the world, and they went out
as quietly as pages torn from a book.

FROM A RUSSIAN PROVERB

Rage all you want. It won't do any good.
We are born in an open meadow
but we die in a dark wood.

You can trace the trouble back to motherhood,
the milk that fed you all those years ago.
Rage all you want. It won't do any good.

The child you were then, so misunderstood,
who hid in leaves shaped to a private burrow,
felt certain we will die in a dark wood.

The father who would not be Robin Hood,
who wouldn't steal, but only borrow,
raged all he wanted. It did no good.

The friends and siblings always ready with a *should*
as if their shame would morph into your sorrow—
they knew, they all knew we die in a dark wood.

You feel it beating in your blood
and turn away until tomorrow.
Rage all you want. It won't do any good.
We die—we all die—in a dark wood.

A KILLING

A man lay bleeding in Bourke Street.
He went to help a stranger
and the stranger stabbed him in the heart.

A man lay bleeding in Bourke Street.
He bled out to his name
like a hero from a book.

But to his friends
the man who lay bleeding was not
a hero from a book.

Even to me he was a man with a face
and a voice, a man
who once served me an apple tart.

His life was both more and less than a name.
Everything that was not a name
and everything that was

leaked out as the man
lay bleeding. Then his name
flew everywhere at once

but the life behind the name,
the life without a name
was gone

back to where it came from,
before the street became a street,
the knife a knife.

EVERY SAILOR IN HOMER

As every sailor in Homer knew
the weather is open to fluke
and temper.

You're at dusk in a sanguine sea,
the sheets slack and oarsmen at rest,
when suddenly

the mainsail bursts and you're keel-over-hull.
It fills and bursts and you're keel-
over-hull

and your lungs are full and your eyes go wide
and you tear at the sea with the sea inside
of you.

O every sailor in Homer knew.
And every farmer who went to bed
in his house

that a wind can slam the house at night,
that shutters can slap the walls till you rise
in a fright

and stumble through the feeling dark
like a blind man shutting his shutters tight
in the dark.

As every farmer in Homer surely knew,
as anyone near the Aegean knew,
the weather

could turn on you. It could turn on you.
And everyone, everyone knew it could turn
on you.

THE GLOWING

And if there were nowhere a home on earth
in the closeness and noise of other people
in the sound of engines and voices
and roads, if there were nowhere a home,
if the sky came in too close through the arms
of the grasping trees if the whole of everything
were muffled could the stillness that ensued
be joy?
            When fish develop fins and moles
develop hands that can dig the cells glow
for the limbs that will move them, so
the word becomes flesh becomes change.
In the stillness at morning the fog at the window
the gull pausing at low tide, the sounds
of what cannot be seen are the rooms
without walls once entered and left.
Even in these old bones the cells glow
for the limbs that will move them out
to the trees in the fog the tide coming in.

AFTERNOON GOING NOWHERE

Only the winter sunlight
striking through the glass and making
a deeper warmth inside the mind,

only the coffee steaming near at hand,
only the clouds, the bright roofs
of the neighbor houses, only

the distant traffic humming and the sound
of schoolyard children like birds
and birds like schoolyard children,

only the unopened book, only
the garden shadows crossing the floor,
only the smell that brings an absent

childhood back, the ant crossing the page,
the housefly rubbing its hands
on the plate of crumbs, only

the wilted perfume of a winter garden,
only the empty chairs, the coiled hose,
the pots of ravaged herbs,

only the warmth as it occurs again, life-giving
on the skin, the hand that holds
the pen, the day withdrawing soon,

only the distant flagless pole,
the musical score of power lines,
the corrugated shed, the hair

on the backs of arms, the same arms
that splashed in the Aegean and the
Tasman Seas, the same

arms that held her body, the same, only
these and all of these in winter light,
so warm, so nearly sleeping.

One Day

Some are retired by a virus,
I by the passage of time,
equally precarious.

I rise in consoling dark
from dreams of a former life,
those decades of work.

I was always too slow
and now my deadline
nobody knows,

not even the moon
that climbed while I slept
and flared out in the Huon

as the wind kicked up
scuddings of shadow
and the last starlight dropped

in the gum tree grove.
There is only one day
for all that we love.

The world has gone quiet,
pensive, afraid,
angry and divided,

and the mountains return
where the animals thrive
and fuel goes unburned

and the markets dive
and it's day, just a day
to be grateful, alive—

alive as contagion,
prescient as grass
whose numbers are legion.

We lived out by the river
where the grass grew long
and the mountains rose up blue
and we sang the salmon song.

The fish swam up the river,
their spawn went out to sea,
and those were all the seasons
known to my family.

The men had gone to war,
were shipped home, some with scars,
some with wads of dollar bills
and their shark-finned cars,

but way out by the river
the grass grew up so long
you could lie down with your lover
and sing the salmon song.

The old ones turned much older,
the young ones moved away,
the snow flew in a blizzard
that blew night into day.

I went beyond the mountains
and dwelt by the roaring combers.
I started talking to the seals,
the whales and all the roamers.

My sons were born in the desert
and like many sons before
when they grew big enough
they went away to war.

I've known life by the river
I've known life by the sea.
I've known the silent desert
for my only company.

The desert was an ocean
and in the distant roar
you hear inside a fossil shell
all that was here before.

I'll go out by the river
and lie down on a stone
where the lizard waits in summer
naked and alone.

If anyone should see me
tell them nothing's wrong.
I'm just that mad old woman
who sings the salmon song.

THE MUD ROOM

His muddy rubber boots
stood in the farmhouse mud room
while he sat in the kitchen,
unshaven, dealing solitaire.

His wife (we called her Auntie)
rolled out dough in the kitchen
for a pie, put up preserves
and tidied, clearing her throat.

They listened to the TV
at six, he with his fingers
fumbling the hearing aids,
she watching the kitchen clock.

Old age went on like that,
a vegetable patch, a horse
some neighbor kept in the barn,
the miles of grass and fences.

After he died his boots
stood muddy in the mud room
as if he'd gone in socks,
softly out to the meadow.

ARE WE STILL HERE?

Between the woodpile and the window
a line of small black ants is moving,
some to the north, some to the south.

Their constant industry is admirable,
as are their manners when they pause
in meeting to exchange a touch.

I must have brought their home inside
for fuel, heating my small house.
And if it burned I too would move

along all points of the compass rose,
touching my neighbors on the path.

A Wren's Weight

A:

The smallest sound—the pulling on of my shoes
or the click shut of the door as I step outside—
interrupts a planetary silence.

The slap and bite of my neighbor's axe echoes.
Perhaps the ashes I will be have learned
already the lessons taught by a breath of wind.

A wren lights on a blade of pampas grass
and does not bend it, while the air is rent
by throaty motorcycles on the road.

No gesture I can make will budge the earth,
no rage for justice, no love or fever of grief
will leave so much as a wren's weight remaining,

but to have seen this day, or tried to see it
just as it is, is all of privilege,
all time alive in the marrow of sunlight.

B:

It's you I accuse, your sin of passivity,
your prayerful nature and your precious wren.

Just when the marching started up again
you retreated to your island, no less

a gated enclave than a rich man's house,
and there you go on about reality.

The eyes of others burn with tears and smoke.
What will you do now? When will you wake up?

Your broken-hearted words won't lift a stone
against the haters, and you write alone.

A:

The wren is back and smaller than a heart,
a flutter feeding among clumps of grass.
The sea and river meet and mix their waters,

but whether this is love or something other
I cannot say. My life is laid down here.
I know the tears. I know the fire and smoke.

Creation and destruction turn the wheel
that we are bound to, like everything that lives.
The sense of danger must not disappear.

B:

There you go, quoting poetry again.
Rage at the state, rage at the criminal class.

You've given up on any sense of justice.
You see nature's change, but not human change,

the incremental need to rearrange
systems of power, the pinnacle of gain.

Let me tell you the names of our new heroes
pulling down the haters and their statues.

Let me show you the bravery of women,
of every gender facing the baton.

A:

I see it too. Let me show you bravery:
a woman, almost blind, who has lost two sons
and the husband she loved most of all her men,

pushes her wheel barrow uphill every day,
moving the rock and soil, at eighty-nine
mucking in dirt to make some beauty grow.

She rolls a cigarette, drinks a glass of wine
and goes back at it, shaping her block of land—
another kind of incremental change.

That's how I see the act of poetry,
as not unlike the echo of her axe,
the smoke from her woodstove heating the house.

I see the courage you describe. Admit
that hers is also courage, and that all
this courage weighs no more than a tiny wren.

Wood

for an anniversary

I have always loved wood,
the smell of it, the grain
under the hand, the sinew
of living wood upright
in its roots, the green
it breathes to the world,
the crazy salad of colors,
blossom and leaf,
and the eyes where branches were,
knots and boles,
the way as Mark said,
men are trees, walking.

My whole heart is walking,
love, to you, on this,
our day of wood,
the grain of us, the rings
remembering, the way
you will feel like time
in my two hands
when I touch you again.

UNDER THE PEPPERMINT GUMS

Under the tall peppermint gums
with rain-dark skin and upraised limbs,
I see her choose her body's way,
pausing to stare out at the gray
of the Huon's water, and beyond
a cloudy wilderness. Now her blond
hair tied in a mop appears,
her eyes that might be full of tears
as they are brimming with the world,
the color of the sea gone cold.
I could be a hunter in a blind
but she's no prey. She's another kind
no one has quite identified,
though doubtless many men have tried.
Enough to love and let her be
between daydreams of sky and sea.

Love Poem

Only life could evolve
these convolutions, fold
and lip, love's blossom,

but of such hardiness
that new life has come
squalling out of it.

Most of the day this beauty
keeps out of sight
and mind, memory's strong musk.

Only in the safety we have made
of dailiness and care
is touch allowed,

and I have bowed before this flower
knowing fully whom
I so admire.

WORDS FOR HERMES

Where will it end?
Night is leaving and it is not night.
The dawn is coming but it is not dawn.
It's something in between. Not yet decided.
Like the old is dying and the new cannot be born.
Like a door you haven't stepped through yet.
Like me. I live in the between.
You know the story. But do you believe it?

It's like a dance, a circle—
turn, counterturn, stand—
but there is no stand. There is no stop,
no still. Not in your world, not in mine.
I'm the conductor god. I escort the dead
to the Underworld. When you receive
their messages, I heard them first.

I am the god of doorways,
of entrances and exits,
passages between. The movement
never stops, it never stops,
but I have seen the Mercy like a pause,
a momentary stasis in the suffering.

Turn now, and go
into the world of hurt.
Indeed, it knows no borders.
Heal. Or try to heal.
I will be back.

PAINTING THE SHED

This accomplishment, this action of hands,
the soles of one's feet bitten by ladder rungs,
thumbs cramped from pushing the brush
into the crevices of old wood,
and the wood itself silvered by weather,
boards held to the good bones of beams
with rusting nails, the wood so obdurate
it breaks drill bits. This is an old marriage
of person and thing. The shed has stood
for a generation and will surely rot one day
or be blown out by the indifferent god
of a bush fire. Yet it stands, completed
and, like everything else, incomplete.
I love the sawdust floor with its possum droppings,
the solid benches covered with paint cans
and all the potential energy of tools—
these shrines to the mysteries of work,
these places of aspiration, left to themselves.

THE GARDEN AND THE LIBRARY

A gardener grows familiar with the dead
and dying, each tree with its way of letting go,
the oak leaves brittle and difficult to heap,
while beech let down their arms to hold the dead.

I knew a daughter once who could not touch
her dying mother's body. I did it for her.
And while the nurse removed the catheter
and turned the corpse, changing the under-sheet,

the daughter wept and missed the miracle.
I watched the speed with which the nurses worked
and wondered when the immigrant embarked,
now that she was so much like a leaf.

She would be more so in the fire, her ashes
raked and gathered, bagged, identified.
And soon we all had wept, but I kept seeing
the body turned like wood, efficiently.

By then my garden had become a book,
and like all books I felt it come apart
each time I read its leaves. It was a tree
of books, a library of spines in tiers,

so many I couldn't know or read them all.
I thought they were alive, or would give life
to me if I could only read them all.
The shelves grew tall as trees, and weighted down

with books of every kind—novels, poetry,
dictionaries of arcana, alphabets
and sciences and stories of adventure—
books I reach for now, and find them gone.

But I'm the one who's gone, the immigrant.
I've crossed the sea and left so many books
behind, and wonder who will touch their spines
and take them down and love them as I did.

I know so little now about the dead,
the clay and rock I garden in, the trees.
Work is a kind of blessed ignorance
in which no task is ever really done.

I think about those nurses, and their speed
and silence in the face of miracles.
I think of all the weeping, all the books
in tiers of shelves. I think of all the leaves.

STARTING WITH ANONYMOUS

Go tell the king the royal court has fallen.
Apollo has lost his lyre and laurel crown,
The rambling spring is now as dry as bone.

Go tell the mountain that a friend is dying.
Go tell the sea. They've seen the dying done
and know it can't be stopped by anyone.

Go find the dream that left you at a loss
with crowded voices you could not explain
muttering darkly that your life was wrong.

Ask the wind about it. Ask the rain.
Did you believe your life would be a song?
Did you believe you would escape the pain?

Go tell a stone that promises were made.
Go tell the night the universe is calling.
Go tell the grass it can resist the spade.

Anonymous you were when you were born.
Anonymous you will be in the end.
Think of the waking light. Think of your friend.

Written in the Sky

Brother, one of us will die
before the other, who will feel
the absence like a missing bone.

The fog will rise up from the firs
until there are no firs, until
the earth itself is dry as bone,

a broken island no ships pass.
What awkward grief betrayed our bond?
It does not matter now. Out here

the passing waters of a lake
we loved, great cedars
and the birds we feel along the bone

the way a paddler pauses in the dawn,
listening, brother,
to the heart of everything.

LAST FLIGHT IN

Even here, sea's edge
at what some call the ends of the earth,
my laptop is "scanning for viruses."

This morning the channel made
by moonlight on the water
was cold as the soul,

and it brought to mind
the other side of this same ocean,
the years it took to bring me here.

It was no time to have a bad cough—
I mean, before I came to this place,
last flight in.

Days in a deserted city
I nursed myself
grew bored of my cooking.

Then it was time, and just in time,
the nearly empty terminal
and the kinds of armor people wore

as they queued at the gates. They looked
for all the world like an evacuation—
but to what?

Repatriation, but to what?
And I, an immigrant,
stateless in a way

but having stated my desire,
homebound in the air to what
some call the ends of the earth.

Still, it was not so difficult,
speaking to the masks,
the hazmat suits

on both sides of the ocean,
people who would wait their turn
and offer a kind word.

I read of rioting crowds
with automatic rifles,
people screaming their rights,

and I read of nurses dying,
the hundred-mile stare
of E. R. doctors,

and I was through my quarantine
with nothing to declare
but love and gratitude.

Even here, my laptop
hunts incessantly
a kind of enemy,

though clouds and moonlight have not heard
anything untoward about the world
of prospering insects

and the birds have not
forgotten how to sing,
here, even here.

FROM A PASSAGE IN MELVILLE

That great America on the other side of the sphere,
Australia, was given to the enlightened world
by the whaleman. After its first blunder-born
discovery by a Dutchman; all other ships long shunned
those shores as pestiferously barbarous;
but the whale-ship touched there.

                      And therein lies
one rub of many. By the light of all the stars,
the light of the dark between them, the lines
and spaces between the lines distinguished by our lives,

the great blubber-covered muscle of a heart
is now a bleeding froth on the brine, the drag-nets
indiscriminately harvesting, the mouths feeding.
How are we to judge our own barbarity?

We who know not what we are
cannot amend ourselves, cannot suspend
the blather of unbelieving, the special habits.
And who alone will be left to tell of this?

Oh, let it go, let all discovery
teach us to love the globe, that troubled child
holding itself while constant anger rages.
We have so little time in which to learn of it.

In future years, if we are lucky, we
might still be known as makers, not destroyers.
We might be seen for what we wished to be,
even as our bones tell other stories.

New Zealand Letter

(Revised in memory of Anne Stevenson, 1933–2020)

Nothing, not even the wind that blows, is so
unstable as the level of the crust of the earth.
—Charles Darwin

This morning, groggy and a bit footsore
from another tramp in these New Zealand hills,
I write to you, Anne and Peter, in Wales
or Durham, no doubt hoofing it yourselves,
or Anne with Mozart at her fingertips,
Peter tracking Darwin across the page.
Just now the sun slipped under laden clouds,
lighting a forest that, from where I sit,
could be some alternate Seattle, made
by an artist fond of Hobbits and Maori lore,
exotic but expected like the sky
two nights ago: Orion on his back,
and at the opposite end what Bishop called
the kite sticks of the Southern Cross.

                         Out here
in Queenstown's alps I'm slightly less at sea.
Two weeks ago, in a Northland port of call
that battened down its hatches while a squall
unsteadied solid earth like a tipped canoe,
I lay awake in a house on Hospital Hill.
The continent of home, familiar, firm,
was far away. I felt, as Freud might say,
that oceanic, vague, religious sense,
my confirmation of insignificance,
and wondered with my hearing aids turned off
how thought would swim if I were totally deaf,
if wind and sails, wails, whales, and even Wales
were all the same descending sonar ping,
an undersea sensation. I thought of friends
like you who sound these depths without the bends.

Forgive this letter from a wanderer.
Forgive the *sound* of this, my sounding out
locations you have yet to see or hear,
and let me tender my small vision here.

Begin with the region's young geology,
the accident of islands that still rise
and spiral into zig-zag mountain ranges,
glaciers long and white as wizards' beards,
cold rivers, silt green or so transparent
they flow like breezes blowing over stones.
Now fill in lichens, mosses, undergrowth
of silver fern and berry-laden shrubs,
the eerie forest of the podocarp,
its leafless branches choked by hanging moss,
rare stands of rimu pine, the nikau palm,
sheep meadows scoured by European gorse—
alpine, tropical and imported plants
tossed on the rumps and hummocks of the land
right down to the shoreline birds, the dotterels,
whimbrels, bar-tailed godwits, white-faced heron
lording like headwaiters at low tide,
the shags and oystercatchers, penguins, grebes.
And here the albatross alights at last,
world traveler folding its weary wings.
Inland, white-backed magpies and pokeko birds
dot meadows, while in woods the begging wekas
pester walkers. Others I need hearing aids
to catch: fantails, bellbirds, twitching finches
chatter in humid shade, guarding their eggs
from possums or the poisons humans spray.

Which brings me around at last to swelling towns
like Auckland, Napier, Christchurch, Wellington,
the tourist hustle, some of it rough as guts,

where Poms and Yanks, Pakehas of all stripes,
mix with Maori and new-wave immigrants,
fractious and varied as the forest birds.
It's like Creation's proud Cloudcuckooland
but earthbound, addled by bungee-jumping youth.
Each permanent or momentary claim
asserts a version of this land or sea
so freshly robbed or its virginity,
where moko hoons mark turf, spray-painting walls,
or clash like rugby teams in free-for-alls.
The spillage of spoiled empires everywhere
rumbles ashore like the redundant surf.

Yet the never-far-off sea still models change
like that wind I started with, to rearrange
Aotearoa, land of the white cloud.
Darwin hated it and only stayed
a week, bound for the sedentary life
that would explore as no one else had done
currents in all species known to the sun.
And terminal cases on every kind of pill
in every weather out on Hospital Hill
can try to see the earth for what it is,
not as the perfect dream that always dies,
the Promised Land promoted in brochures,
but as the sort of matter that endures
by changing.

              Some of its forms we recognize.
Others astonish—the inarticulate
we try to voice before it is too late,
this metamorphic world, tidal and worn,
rooted, adrift, alive, and dying to be born.

Antipodes

in memory of Derek Mahon, 1941–2020

The death of the poet tenders a new start,
one's own slate of errors wiped clean, and the day
contributes a close horizon bound in fog.

This could be Ireland with its smear of rain.
English lies on Tasmania, a light veneer
of colonial regret and gratitude,

while ghostly gum trees stand against the white
like muted ancestors at a loss for words.
What should one do on such a day but write?

Our garden sequined with raindrops could be
the churchyard where you stood with Seamus and Mike,
young poets at a poet's unmarked grave.

What you felt for MacNeice I feel for you.
THIS MAN WITH THE SHY SMILE HAS LEFT BEHIND
SOMETHING THAT WAS INTACT—those are the words

now carved on the headstone in Carrowdore,
like all words belonging to no one. Still,
what a thing to have done with one's imperfect life.

BIOGRAPHIA LITERARIA

in memory of Alastair Reid, 1926–2014

Some men I knew, a strange connection, rain
as if a shell exploded in the cosmos.
You'd think we were old friends met after fighting.

And here's a brain to reassemble, cells
and ashes fallen in reminding weather.
Whimsy and effort of their lives, the women

known to men I knew in another life,
and I have somehow to make sense of it—
the expeditionary words, the poems,

gravity of Merwin, delight of Graves,
delinquent me caught up in all the stories.
Your papers, please. As I approach the border.

Note to Self

To be old and not to feel it is a gift.
To be supplanted and not to care. So be it.
The birds are not supplanted by the air,
the air, what's left of it, by flood or fire.

The effort of a life, the wasted hour,
the kind word given to a stranger's child
are understood as kin and disappear.
Time to be grass again. Ongoing. Wild.

David Mason grew up in Bellingham, Washington and has lived in many parts of the world, including Greece and Colorado, where he served as poet laureate for four years. His books of poems began with *The Buried Houses, The Country I Remember*, and *Arrivals*. His verse novel, *Ludlow*, was named best poetry book of the year by the *Contemporary Poetry Review* and the National Cowboy & Western Heritage Museum. It was also featured on the *PBS NewsHour*. He has written a memoir and four collections of essays. His poetry, prose, and translations have appeared in such periodicals as the *New Yorker, Harper's Magazine, The Nation, The New Republic*, the *New York Times*, the *Wall Street Journal*, the *Times Literary Supplement, Poetry*, and the *Hudson Review*. Anthologies include *Best American Poetry, The Penguin Anthology of Twentieth-Century American Poetry*, and others. He has also written libretti for operas by Lori Laitman and Tom Cipullo, all available on CD from Naxos. In 2015 Mason published two poetry collections: *Sea Salt: Poems of a Decade* and *Davey McGravy: Tales to Be Read Aloud to Children and Adult Children*. *The Sound: New and Selected Poems* and *Voices, Places: Essays* appeared in 2018. *Incarnation and Metamorphosis: Can Literature Change Us?* will appear in 2023. He lives with his wife Chrissy (poet Cally Conan-Davies) in Tasmania on the edge of the Southern Ocean.

CPSIA information can be obtained
at www.ICGtesting.com
Printed in the USA
LVHW041238130722
723005LV00001B/1

9 781636 280578